# TAROT FOR BEGINNERS

## AN INTRODUCTORY GUIDE TO USING TAROT FOR PERSONAL GROWTH

### REAL WORLD TAROT BOOKS

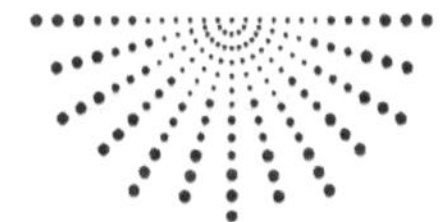

## KAT ELMWOOD

SEEKERS GROVE PRESS

# CONTENTS


*Introduction*                                          vii
*Who Is This Book Not For*                              xi

## UNDERSTANDING TAROT

TAROT GLOSSARY                                          3

THE COMPONENTS OF A TAROT DECK                          7
Major Arcana                                            7
Minor Arcana                                            8
Court Cards                                             9

SYMBOLISM IN TAROT                                      10
The Elements                                            10
Colors                                                  11
Animals                                                 11
Landscapes and Locations                                12
Objects                                                 13
Figure Positions                                        13
Minor Arcana Suit Names                                 14
Gender                                                  14
Numbers                                                 16
The Court Figures                                       18
Jungian Archetypes                                      19

COMMON TAROT MISCONCEPTIONS                             26
Myth - Your First Tarot Deck Should Be A Gift
From Someone Else                                       26
Myth - You Can't Read Tarot For Yourself                27
Myth - Tarot Predicts the Future                        28
Myth - Only Psychics Can Read Tarot                     28
Myth - Tarot is Associated with Evil/The Devil          29
Myth - Each Card Has a Fixed Meaning                    29
Myth - Tarot Readings Should Always Be
Positive                                                29
Myth - Card Meanings Are Literal                        30
Myth - Tarot Readings Are Quick Fixes                   30

Myth - Tarot Can Control or Manipulate   30

Myth - You Must Follow A Certain Religion or
Spiritual Tradition To Use Tarot   31

Myth - Tarot Has Rules   31

Myth - Oracle and Tarot Decks Are The Same
Thing   32

IS TAROT MAGICAL?   33

## USING TAROT

CHOOSING A TAROT DECK   37

The Rider-Waite-Smith Deck (RWS)   37

How To Choose A Deck   38

Where To Buy Tarot Cards?   39

Caring For Your Cards   39

Bonding Through Regular Readings   42

Creating a Tarot Reading Space   42

Shuffling   44

CONSULT THE BOOKS OR LEARN THE
CARDS FROM MEMORY?   45

INTUITIVE READING   47

How To Do An Intuitive Reading   47

Mindfulness and Intuitive Reading   48

Combining Tradition and Intuition   49

Embracing Other's Interpretations   49

Getting Started With Intuitive Reading   49

WHAT CAN TAROT BE USED FOR?   50

Self-Reflection   50

Asking Questions   50

Recognizing Emotional Patterns   51

Tarot Journaling   51

Integrating Tarot into Meditation and
Mindfulness   52

Setting Intentions with Tarot   52

MAKING DECISIONS WITH TAROT   54

Yes No Answers   55

GOAL SETTING AND PLANNING WITH
TAROT                                                    56
Clarifying Your Goals                                    56
Reflecting on Motivations                                57
Identifying Strengths and Challenges                     58
Visualization and Manifestation                          58
Creating Inspired Action Plans                           59
Adapting to Change and Flexibility                       59
Recognizing Achievements                                 60

TAROT FOR CREATIVE INSPIRATION                           61
Uncovering Your Creativity                               61
Exploring Your Creativity                                62
Working with Existing Creative Projects                  62
Creating Creative Rituals                                63

WORKING WITH TRADITIONAL SPREADS                         65
The Celtic Cross                                         66
Three Card Spreads                                       69
The Horseshoe Spread                                     70

CREATING YOUR OWN TAROT SPREADS                          72
WHAT TO DO WHEN A TAROT READING
DOESN'T FEEL RIGHT                                       74
TAROT READER'S BLOCK                                     76
Continuing Your Tarot Journey                            78

*The Real World Tarot Books Series by Kat Elmwood*       81
*About The Author*                                       83

# INTRODUCTION

Tarot isn't just a deck of cards with pretty pictures that mean things. Tarot is a mirror reflecting the depths of your subconscious. Tarot is a storyteller weaving tales of past, present, and future. Tarot is a tool that empowers you to tap into your intuition and gain clarity in a chaotic world. It is a companion on your journey through this wild life.

For centuries, curious minds have looked to the tarot to find meaning and direction. Anything with such a rich and esoteric, occult history is naturally going to be shrouded in veils of mystery. This book pulls back those veils in simple, no nonsense ways, demystifying tarot's symbolism, expelling its myths, and equipping you with the skills to embark on your own exciting voyages of insight with this remarkable tool as your compass.

## CONVERSATIONS WITH TAROT

Reading tarot is a conversation with your inner wisdom. The images on the cards are a language that speaks to your soul and your subconscious, providing guidance, encouragement, and sometimes a gentle nudge in the right direction. To learn to read tarot, all you need to do is to learn that language.

The language of tarot is not a secret known only to select people with "special powers." The language of tarot is available to anyone, no matter who you are, no matter what literal language you speak, no matter your age, culture, or spiritual beliefs. The language of tarot can change, ebb and flow and evolve from reader to reader and deck to deck. Tarot, like any language, is a living thing. This book will teach you how to use that language and have deep and meaningful conversations with your deck.

## LEARNING TO READ TAROT

You do not need any special training or innate skills to read tarot. All that is required is a deck, an open heart, and a curiosity about the magic that lives within everyone.

This book is just the tip of the iceberg when it comes to learning tarot. No tarot reader ever gets to the bottom of that iceberg. There is always more to learn, always a new deck, a new symbol, and a new interpretation. You are always growing, your life experiences always changing, and your conversation with tarot will grow and develop along with you. That said, there are a few pieces of entry level information that will help you get going with confidence, and there is enough in this book so that, even if you've never picked up a deck before, you can get into a deep and enlightening reading for yourself or for others.

Are you ready to begin your captivating journey into the world of divination, self-discovery, and intuitive exploration?

WHO AM I?

I am a writer, a mother, a wife, a friend, an artist, and a seeker, a regular woman who lives in a never tidy enough suburban house and watches TV every day, does school runs, goes to the gym, and walks the dog. It's all very ordinary stuff and only a few people in my everyday life know of my relationship with tarot.

For decades, tarot has accompanied me through all of my life stages, from leaving home, college, relationships, marriage, parenthood, career changes, creative projects, and everything in between.

My relationship with tarot began as a teenager, when a simple introductory tarot pamphlet ignited a spark within me, a spark that grew into a flame that continues to burn some three decades later.

Without the means back then to buy a deck of my own, I made one, copying the Rider-Waite-Smith images as best as my limited drawing skills allowed. This was long before the internet, and I only had access to pictures of the Majors, so the Minor cards remained a mystery, prompting me to craft my own pip designs. Today, that homemade deck and the satin bag I hand sewed to protect it remain cherished possessions alongside my many commercial tarot decks.

For me, tarot serves as a powerful moment to step away from a world dominated by skepticism and productivity. It allows me the space to tap into something slower, more beautiful, and often contrary to societal norms. While I do, at times, attach to tarot's occult associations, my connection to the cards roots in the magic of emotions, personal power, intuition, and intentional manifestation.

It's my honor to share this magic with you so that you too can ignite tarot's spark of wisdom and carry it to illuminate your path.

# WHO IS THIS BOOK NOT FOR

This book is not suitable for every person interested in tarot.

If you're out to find a fast lesson in fortune-telling with guaranteed lottery numbers, or to know what someone is thinking, this might not be the guide for you. This book is not a shortcut to fame, fortune, mind-reading, or solving all of life's mysteries in a single spread.

If you're looking for a strict set of rules, you may find my flexible approach to tarot is not for you.

If you prefer a purely logical approach to understanding the world, the intuitive, symbolic, and sometimes magical realm of tarot might not align with your expectations.

If you are uncomfortable exploring the depths of your own emotions or resist the idea of personal growth, the transformative power of tarot might not be in your interest.

This journey is for those who embrace uncertainty, relish in the beauty of the endless questions of the universe, are in tune with their inner knowing, and are open to the endless possibilities that the tarot can unfold.

# UNDERSTANDING TAROT

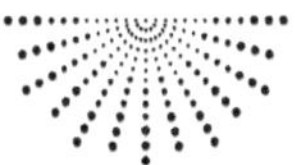

# TAROT GLOSSARY

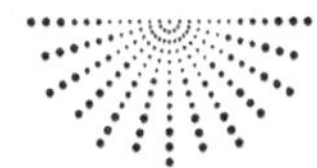

Tarot cards are a rich language in themselves, and the tarot community also talks about the practice in certain ways. This glossary provides a foundational understanding of tarot's essential elements. Some terms may be self-explanatory, others entirely new. Use this list as a quick, easy access guide, and see the following section, The Components of A Tarot Deck, for further details.

**Arcana**
The term "arcana" literally means secrets or mysteries. Tarot decks comprise two main sections, called the Arcanas: Major Arcana and Minor Arcana.

**Clarifier Card**
An optional card drawn during a reading to provide further insights into specific issues, or to deepen understanding of existing cards in the spread.

**Court Cards**
Found in the Minor Arcana, these cards—Page, Knight,

Queen, and King—represent various personality types or archetypes at different stages of learning. Court cards may indicate specific individuals or aspects of an individual's personality.

## Deck

A collection of tarot cards unified by a theme, artistic style, or other cohesive elements. Modern decks typically have seventy-eight cards, drawing inspiration from the iconic Rider-Waite-Smith deck. Many individuals select decks that resonate with their personality and interests.

## Intuitive Reading

The personal interpretations of a card's meaning, drawn from the reader's life experiences and intuition. Intuitive readings consider the card's imagery, position in the spread, and the reader's innate reaction to any card.

## Major Arcana

Made up of twenty-two cards (numbered 0-21), the Major Arcana symbolizes significant life moments, fate, major personality traits, and existential themes. Each card follows a narrative akin to the hero's journey, beginning with the innocent Fool (0), navigating through various strengths and trials, and emerging as a wiser individual in the World (21).

## Minor Arcana

Representing day-to-day events, emotions, and less profound situations, the Minor Arcana consists of four suits: Cups, Swords, Pentacles, and Wands. Each suit embodies distinct themes and contains thirteen cards, including Court cards (Page, Knight, Queen, King) and numbered cards (Ace through Ten). Different decks may call their Minor suits by different names.

## Pip Cards

Simple symbolic representations lacking elaborate artwork, akin to the designs in a standard deck of playing cards.

## Querent

The individual for whom a tarot reading is conducted. When reading for oneself, the reader assumes both roles: reader and querent. When reading for others, the person receiving the reading is the querent.

## Reversals

The orientation of a card—upright or reversed—can alter its meaning. While some readers focus solely on upright interpretations, others explore the shadowy nuances offered by reversed cards, perceiving them as negative or indicative of blocked energies. Many tarot practitioners look at reversals as messages from the shadow self.

## Rider-Waite-Smith (RWS) Deck

First published in 1909, the Rider-Waite-Smith tarot deck is the standard from which most modern decks draw upon. The name of the deck is derived from the publisher, The Rider Company, and the author, A.E. Waite, who set out his intentions for the deck design and wrote the original explanatory guidebook. For many years, Pamela Coleman Smith, the artist responsible for the now iconic imagery, went largely uncredited. Indeed, it is most common to see this deck referred to as simply the Rider-Waite deck. More and more in the tarot community are now rightly exploring and acknowledging Smith's vital contribution and thereby rename the deck the Rider-Waite-Smith deck.

## Significator

A card chosen to represent the querent at the time of the reading. While typically a deliberate selection, it can also be

selected randomly. Drawing a Significator card is not
mandatory unless specified by the spread.

**Spreads**
Patterns in which cards are laid out during a reading, with
each position conveying specific meanings. Many tarot
readers begin with traditional spreads and develop their own
over time.

**Suits**
The four divisions of the Minor Arcana—Wands, Cups,
Swords, and Pentacles—each with its unique themes and
symbolism. The suits equate to the suits of regular playing
cards: clubs, hearts, spades, and diamonds.

**Traditional Meaning**
Each tarot card carries a conventional interpretation, often
reflected symbolically in its artwork.

# THE COMPONENTS OF A TAROT DECK

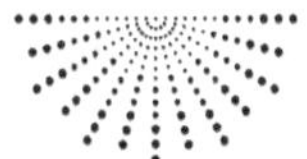

The standard tarot deck is made up of multiple components. Understanding the basic elements of a tarot deck is fundamental to learning its profound symbolism and interpreting its messages.

## MAJOR ARCANA

The Major Arcana comprises twenty-two cards numbered from 0 to 21. Each card in the Major Arcana represents a powerful archetype or universal theme, encapsulating the journey of the human experience from innocence to enlightenment. These are the cards that most tarot newcomers are familiar with, usually through popular culture. They have titled names including The High Priestess, Death, The Devil, The Tower, The Sun, The Moon, The Empress, etc.

The Major Arcana represents the narrative journey of a person through their life. It starts with the Fool (0) in the leaning position, and moves through various stages of the acquisition of wisdom and experience, until finally arriving at the pinnacle of knowledge in The World card (21). It is important to note here that the Fool card is not number one, but rather is numbered as the zero card. As such, the Fool sits at both the beginning and the end of a life cycle. There is always more knowledge to attain, another cycle to embark on, and we are always at some point in this cycle, both the Fool and the World simultaneously.


MINOR ARCANA

In contrast to the sweeping themes of the Major Arcana, the Minor Arcana delves into the nuances of everyday life, illuminating the ebbs and flows of human existence. Typically comprising fifty-six cards divided into four suits—Cups, Swords, Pentacles, and Wands—the Minor Arcana mirrors the diverse facets of human experience, from emotions, and intellect, to material concerns, and creative endeavors.

Each suit within the Minor Arcana embodies a distinct realm of existence, offering insight into the challenges, triumphs, and lessons encountered on the journey of self-discovery.

> **Cups** - Emotions, relationships, intuition, creativity
> and the realm of the heart.
> **Swords** - Intellect, thoughts, communication, conflict,
> and mental clarity.
> **Pentacles** - Material aspects of life. Finances, security,
> physical health. Also commonly called Coins.
> **Wands** - Inspiration, creation, manifestation, passion,
> ambition, and spiritual growth.

Different decks may have different names for these suits. For example, I have seen decks that refer to Pentacles as Shields, Wands and Spears, Cups as Chalices, etc. This is explored further in the following section on tarot symbolism.

Each suit of the Minor Arcana has its Court cards. These are the Page, Knight, Queen, and King. The Court cards represent distinct facets of human nature, personifying the myriad roles and personas we embody throughout our lives.

**Page** - Youthful exuberance and ideals.
**Knight** - Acting on those ideals with gusto.
**Queen** - The pinnacle manifestation of feminine energies and wisdoms.
**King** - The pinnacle manifestation of masculine energies and wisdoms.

Some believe that the King outranks the Queen, a higher manifestation of learning. I prefer to see them as equals at opposite ends of the same energy spectrum. We look at Court cards further in the following section on Symbolism.

# SYMBOLISM IN TAROT

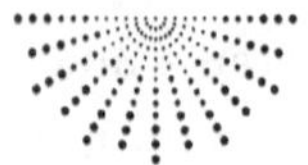

Tarot is a language of symbols. While every deck will employ unique symbolism according to its art, understanding overall general symbols to be on the lookout for when learning tarot can help you gain a deeper affinity with the cards.

This section covers some of the basic symbols of the tarot, as well as the complex symbolisms of gender, more details of what the Court cards mean, numerology, and Jungian archetypes.

## THE ELEMENTS

The four suits in the tarot Minor Arcana correspond to the four classical elements: fire, water, air, and earth. These elemental forces infuse each suit with distinct qualities.

**Fire - Wands**
Wands embody the fiery energy of passion and creativity, enthusiasm, and motivation.
**Water - Cups**
Cups resonate with the emotional depths of water and

talk about emotional undercurrents of relationships with ourselves and with others.

**Air - Swords**

Swords symbolize the ethereal domain of thoughts, communication, as well as conflict.

**Earth - Pentacles**

Pentacles ground us in the earthly, material world of employment, financial matters, our physical bodies, material possessions and everything that keeps us rooted in day-to-day reality.


COLORS

The color palette in a tarot deck is typically intentional, with each hue carrying its own symbolic weight. The reds and oranges can symbolize passion and action, while blues speak to emotions, intuition, and communication. Grays often represent the intellect and clarity of thought. Greens and browns speak to material aspects and grounded energy. These are the most common symbolic uses of color, but each deck will take its own unique approach.


ANIMALS

Animals are another symbolic language frequently employed in tarot. The ways animals are used are many and variable. Dogs can mean domesticity, while wolves can be our wild nature. We see this most classically in The Moon card of the RWS deck. This card also shows off a lobster emerging from the water, symbolizing our primal subconsciousness.

Fish speak to undercurrents and depths of wisdom, lions to power, foxes to cunning, cats to the spiritual realm. The Strength card of RWS traditions depicts a woman wrestling with a lion to indicate a wild force being brought under control by inner powers.

The Wheel of Fortune RWS card shows a variety of animals. The sphinx represents the mysteries of life. Sphinxes are also featured on The Chariot card to a similar effect. The jackal, which is traditionally associated with Anubis, represents the cycle of life from death to rebirth. In each corner of the card, we see four creatures: an ox, a lion, an eagle, and a human. These represent the four evangelists of the Christian gospel. Matthew is the man, Mark is the lion, the ox is Luke, and the eagle is John. These symbols are also connected to the fixed astrological symbols, Aquarius, Taurus, Leo, and Scorpio.

The list of potential totemic animals is endless and every deck will portray animals to different effects, if they are used at all.

When considering what the appearance of an animal in a reading may symbolize, consider also your personal associations with that animal. For example, for some, a cat is homely comfort, for others it's a wild nature. It might also represent both, existing simultaneously in the one being.


## LANDSCAPES AND LOCATIONS

The world around us also comes into play in the symbolic language of the tarot. Mountains can mean struggles, forests can mean the subconscious. Deserts and wastelands represent barrenness and lack, whereas orchards and gardens symbolize security and abundance.

Houses can represent stability and home life. Cities might talk to community and the hubbub of the busy world. Sacred buildings like churches may also appear, speaking of insight, sanctuary, or institutional traditions.

OBJECTS

The symbolic objects that might appear in a tarot deck are infinite. Yet here are a few of the more obvious symbolic items to keep an eye out for.

Flowers could be beauty, and fruit can be abundance or fertility. Headwear, particularly crowns, as well as scepters, speaks to earthly power. The object representations of the four suits (Cups, Wands, Pentacles/Coins, Swords) also come into play in symbology.

How object symbols appear in your deck ultimately depends on the artist and the theme.

When learning your deck, it can be a good idea to create your own reference list. Take up your cards and go through the whole pack, or just a card or two to start, and list all the objects you see and what they might represent within the wider meaning of each card. You can lean on the traditional meanings of the cards or your own intuitive responses.


FIGURE POSITIONS

How a person pictured on the card is positioned can also influence what that figure symbolizes. For example, a figure turning away might mean something is hidden or being avoided, or a figure square on might show power, strength, or determination.

You can also look to positional figures in your readings as a whole, examining how figures might interact from card to card. For example, you might see the away facing figure on the Ten of Wands (a card traditionally meaning the burden of hard work) to be turning away from the forward facing and quite jaunty Two of Pentacles (a card about juggling and balance in a materialistic sense). Perhaps this pairing is a warning that the querent is turning away from the juggle required to do a particular work.

The names of the Minor Arcana suits can vary from deck to deck, and this can alter the symbolism of the cards in that deck. For example, sometimes Pentacles is called Coins. "Pentacles" brings the cards into the realm of the mystic, referencing the pentacle used in many Pagan spiritual practices. "Coins", on the other hand, takes the cards more literally into the world of money and materialism. Cups are sometimes also called Chalices. While a "cup" could mean any kind of vessel, even an ordinary water tumbler, a chalice is something far more luxurious, perhaps even with ritualistic overtones.

In one of my favorite decks (*Legend: The Arthurian Tarot,* by Anna Marie Ferguson) Pentacles are replaced by Shields. This gives the cards another layer of symbolism, as we might be prompted to consider the protective roles of these cards. In the same deck, Wands are called Spears, making the traditional actionable manifestations of the suit take on a more forceful nature. Of course, these suit changes are intended to suit the medieval chivalry theme of the deck as a whole.

If you find yourself with a deck that plays with the suits' names, consider the deck's theme to infer deeper symbolic nature of the individual Minor cards.


GENDER

Within the standard Rider-Waite-Smith inspired decks, several cards carry gendered titles such as Priestess, Emperor, and Empress. Additionally, certain cards traditionally depict gendered representations. For example, The Hermit and The Magician often show a male figure, while The Moon and The Star frequent a female representation.

Not all decks have these gendered figures. Some depict all

women, some have all men, some have queer and trans figures, some decks have entirely gender neutral cards.

Gender in the cards does not specifically pertain to scientifically assigned distinctions between male and female. The energies represented in these cards refer to the broader energetic spectrum of the masculine and the feminine. In Jungian terms, this is equated with the animus/anima archetype spectrum. There is more on Jungian archetypes in the following section.

The masculine or animus energy aligns with the physical and earthly, while the feminine or anima energies are associated with the emotional, psychological, and spiritual realms. Masculine energy is externally powerful. It is a confrontational energy. Feminine energy is inward facing. It is emotionally and intuitively powerful.

It's crucial to note that these energies can coexist within the same card, just as they coexist in the same person, regardless of their scientifically assigned sex. For instance, The Hermit card typically portrays a male figure, yet its essence delves into a feminine energy, symbolizing a retreat for emotional, psychological pondering, healing, and replenishment.

Throughout this book, and all books in my tarot series, I employ traditionally gendered pronouns based on the representations in the decks I am using for demonstration. For instance, when discussing the RWS Magician, I will use "he." However, it's crucial to understand that this discussion revolves around energy and personality, operating within a cyclical spectrum.

If my use "he" or "she" does not align with your identity or beliefs, please recognize it as a shorthand for masculine or feminine energies. I am not using traditional gender pronouns to reference biological sex or any binary gender identifications.

NUMBERS

Numbers play a significant role in tarot symbolism, adding deeper layers of meaning to the cards.

Throughout the deck, each number is ascribed a certain symbolic value.

It's up to the individual reader how deeply they want to go into tarot numerology. Some readers are perfectly fine without interpreting numerology at all, but if you're interested in learning, the following is a basic introduction of what numbers represent in the cards, particularly the Minor Arcana.

**Odds and Evens**

Some believe that, across the Minor Arcana, even numbers align with feminine energy and odd numbers with the masculine.

**Ace**

Ace is an interesting numerical position in playing cards because, like the tarot's 0 Fool card, it can come at the beginning or at the end of the numerical sequence, depending on the game. In the Minor Arcana, the Ace is most often understood as the 1 card.

Aces herald something new with expansive potential. Aces are typically the pure energy of what their suit represents. While Aces contain strength and vibrancy, this raw potential can harm if not tempered accordingly.

**Twos**

The twos introduce the theme of coming together in pairs, encapsulating the complexities of unions. Transitioning from the individuality of ones, twos are all about harmony and merging of forces to create a cohesive whole.

**Threes**
Tarot threes bring about group dynamics, portraying the potential for diverse outcomes when individuals or ideas unite. Threes can signal the initial culmination of a phase or a project.

**Fours**
Fours suggest the beginnings of advancement after the foundational phases of development have been completed.

**Fives**
Five cards are typically all about change, fluctuations, and potential conflict. Fives prompt introspection, urging us to explore deeper reasons for progress.

**Sixes**
Sixes symbolize the transition away from the turmoil of the fives towards a resolution. It might be internal or external. Sixes represent overcoming suffering and finding light after darkness.

**Sevens**
Seven is an important mystical number and the appearance of a seven card signals a time for introspection and evaluation of our current path.

**Eights**
Eights signify worldly or emotional achievements. We might not have arrived on the path we were expecting, but a new phase of completion or growth is occurring.

**Nines**

Nines signify almost total completion. While the feeling of accomplishment is present, it often requires as a brief pause before the final stage of the cycle unfolds.

**Tens**

With the ten cards, cycles have completed and come full circle. This denotes that from this point onward, new beginnings can be embraced.

When reading your spreads, observe for any apparent patterns. Take notice of the numbers that hold greater prominence. The repetition of numbers could show a necessity to focus on a particular facet of your life, or the recurrence of a specific issue appearing in various forms.

THE COURT FIGURES

As we've already briefly covered, the Court cards are the four figures at the end of each Minor Arcana suit. They are the Page, Knight, Queen, and King.

The Court cards don't really follow that narrative of birth to completion cycle we have in the Ace through ten Minor cards. It's more that they represent different aspects of the suit.

Some think of these as being like personality traits of the suit. Others think of it as more like a progressive development through ranks.

The Court cards, even though they appear as figures, need not represent specific people in the querent's life. It's possible they do, of course, but they could also be all about personality traits, philosophies, or general life stages.

**Page**

The most youthful member of the Court, the Page approaches the suit's energies with curiosity and playfulness. In this sense, he's rather like The Fool. While still in the process of learning about the nature of his suit, the Page engages with its elements with a fresh mind and no judgements. The dark side of the Page is that he is naïve and might not be seeing the entire picture.

## Knights

Knights are a bit like teenagers. They're keen, powerful, smart, and know a fair bit about the world. But the Knights are still youthful and still learning. Knights are noble and strong, they do good work, and are capable of great things, but they are prone to recklessness and imbalance without proper guidance.

## Queens

Queens are the ultimate feminine energy of their suits. They are all about creation and inward reflection and wisdom, and take their power from an inner source.

## Kings

Kings are the ultimate masculine energies of their suits. Kings are outwardly focused and exert power and control through the leadership of others.

## JUNGIAN ARCHETYPES

Archetypes are universal symbols and patterns that resonate across cultures and eras. They are primal systems of thought that are so ingrained in our subconscious that they appear instinctive. Tarot uses archetypes to represent fundamental human experiences, emotions, and themes.

Pioneer psychiatrist and psychoanalyst, Carl Jung developed a system of archetypes of human personality in order to provide insight into the human psyche, allowing us to more fully know ourselves and others on every level. Jungian archetypal theories continue to be used in some psychoanalytical as well as spiritual fields and are a popular tool for dream analysis. While there are numbered lists of groupings of Jungian archetypes around, and certain notable principal archetypes, the number of archetypes is technically limitless.

Tarot uses archetypal symbols as mirrors, reflecting our collective consciousness and experiences, and providing a framework through which we can understand and navigate our own lives. Any card, just like any person, can simultaneously embody a multitude of archetypes.

The following offers a quick overview of some Jungian archetypes and a selection of cards associated with that state. Jungian theory is a massive field and well beyond the scope of this brief book, so I offer the following as a simple primer into ideas you can take into your tarot reading journey.

**A Selection of Jungian Archetypes And Associated Tarot Cards**

**Anima/Animus**
This is the feminine/masculine energy spectrum referenced in previous sections. The animus embodies the outward facing "masculine" facets of our character. It symbolizes an inclination towards observation, rationality, and the construction of logical frameworks. This contrasts with the intuitive and profound emotional inner nature of the "femi-

nine" anima. We all have both within us operating on an ebb and flow along this energetic spectrum.

The Lovers - Anima/Animus
The High Priestess - Anima
The Hierophant - Animus
The Moon - Anima
Strength - Anima/Animus
The Chariot - Animus
The Emperor - Animus
The Empress - Anima
Temperance - Anima/Animus
Kings - Animus
Queens – Anima
Cups – Anima
Swords - Animus

**The Child/Innocent**
The child or innocent archetype strives for safety and happiness. They yearn to evade harm and wrongdoing. The innocent is optimistic and operates heavily on faith.
The Fool
Aces
Pages

**The Creator**
Creators strive to craft enduring creations and manifest visions. A creator holds authenticity and imagination in high esteem.
The Magician
Wands

**The Every Person**
The every person archetype craves connections and a sense of belonging, esteeming down-to-earth authenticity and equity, and interpersonal bonds.

The Minor Arcana
Seven of Cups
Ten of Pentacles

**The Explorer**
Explorers strive to comprehend the world and their role
within it, cherishing autonomy, ambition, and authenticity.
The Knights
The Hanged Man

**The Father**
A paternal leader of others, and a forceful protector.
The Emperor
The Hierophant
Kings

**Hero**
Heroes seek validation through courageous feats and over-
coming challenges. The hero aspires to wield their mastery
for the betterment of the world.
Knights
The Chariot
Strength
Judgement
Justice

**The Jester**
The jester revels in the present moment, finding joy in
humor and play while uplifting others.
The Fool
Pages
Two of Pentacles

**The Lover**
The lover pursues intimacy and experiences steeped in love.

They are preoccupied with relationships and personal
fulfillment.
The Lovers
Cups

## The Magician
Magicians aspire to manifest dreams into reality and reshape
existence. They honor knowledge and revere the underlying
laws of the universe.
The Magician
Aces

## The Mother
The mother devotes herself to aiding and shielding others.
Often, mothers prioritize their needs above their own.
The Empress
Queens

## The Persona
The persona is the version of ourselves that we seek to
control, the public face of our nature that we put out into the
world.
The Magician
Wands
Judgement

## The Rebel
Rebels yearn for radical change and upheaval of the status
quo. The Rebel archetype is prepared to dismantle anything
that fails to function.
The Hanged Man
Knights
The Tower
Five of Swords

**The Ruler**
The ruler craves control and aims to foster prosperity within their family or community. Rulers seek success and stability above all else.
The Emperor
The Empress
The Chariot
Strength
Kings
Queens

**The Sage (Wise Old Man/Woman)**
The sage, or wise old man/woman, archetype quests for truth and enlightenment. Sages hold wisdom and intellect in supreme value.
The High Priestess
The Hierophant
The Hermit
Queens
Kings

**The Self**
The Self represents a unification of all the archetypes within the whole person.
The World
Judgement
The Court cards

**The Shadow**
The shadow is that side of human nature that operates behind the scenes, below the status quo. The shadow isn't necessarily evil, bad, or wrong, but it is simply the hidden parts of ourselves that subconsciously direct our motivations. The shadow can be something we hide intentionally from others, or it might also refer to aspects of the Self that

our subconscious hides from us as well. This can, of course, be "bad" qualities, but it might also be things like a subconscious drive to be good, a subconscious drive to provide value, and so on.
The Devil
Death
The Tower
The Moon

# COMMON TAROT MISCONCEPTIONS

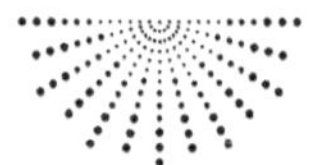

Any tradition so old, so entwined with magic and mysticism, is going to have misconceptions attached to it about how to use the cards, what they mean, and who is permitted to use them.

In this chapter, we debunk some of the most prevalent tarot misconceptions.

## MYTH - YOUR FIRST TAROT DECK SHOULD BE A GIFT FROM SOMEONE ELSE

A myth has taken root that suggests your first tarot deck should be a gift from someone else.

Some believe that a tarot deck carries the energy of the giving, and therefore makes the deck more potent for the reader recipient. While the sentiment behind this notion is charming, it's not true, and prevents many tarot curious people from getting started.

A significant aspect of tarot is the personal connection between the reader and the cards. Choosing your own deck allows you to connect with the imagery, symbolism, and energy on a deeply personal level. When you select your own tarot deck, you are more likely to resonate with the artwork, themes, and overall aesthetic, fostering a stronger and more authentic connection.

Tarot is a tool for self-reflection, guidance, and personal growth. While it's sure is nice to receive a deck as a gift, not receiving one should not restrict your ability to explore and embrace the tradition.

You are allowed to buy your own tarot deck.

Embrace the freedom to choose a deck that speaks to you, allowing your intuition and personal connection to guide your selection. Remember, the magic of tarot lies in the authentic and personal relationship you cultivate with the cards and the practice. So, please, give yourself the gift of your first deck.


## MYTH - YOU CAN'T READ TAROT FOR YOURSELF

This is a question I get asked all the time.

"Can I read tarot for myself?"

The answer is a confident YES!

You absolutely can read tarot for yourself, and doing so is an immensely rewarding journey of self-discovery.

When you read for yourself, profound introspection is possible. Reading for yourself creates a direct line between your psyche and the cards. Often the meanings of a spread are an immediate gut knowing that do not need to be unraveled by analyzing the cards one by one or even a full articulation of thought.

Some questions, particularly those laden with intense emotions or requiring impartial judgment, may benefit from the detached viewpoint of a secondary reader. If you can have your cards read by someone else, go for it. But it doesn't always have to be that way. Indeed, reading for yourself creates an intimacy with the tarot that experiencing the cards through someone else can never bring.

This intimacy, however, comes with the responsibility of maintaining objectivity. Familiarity with the cards might breed assumptions, and emotional investments may influence interpretations. As such, self-awareness is critical in solo tarot practice. Be aware of when you are speaking for the cards and when they are speaking to you.

To mitigate these challenges, many self-readers establish rituals for grounding and clarity.

I don't believe it's possible to have a truly unbiased reading. Our intuitions are always going to come into our conversations with the cards, but we must strive to remain open to what they are telling us, even when, and *especially* when, we disagree with what has been drawn.


## MYTH - TAROT PREDICTS THE FUTURE

Many people, typically those who have not used cards before, believe tarot cards have the power to predict the future. In reality, tarot is a tool for guidance and self-reflection, not a magical crystal ball. Sure, some things that the tarot might label as a future forecast might come to pass. This is because when we infer the future from a reading, it is usually a prediction based on the patterns of what came before, not a moment of psychic foresight. Not that this kind of magical divination is impossible (I claim nothing is impossible!). This is just the way it happens for most of us.


## MYTH - ONLY PSYCHICS CAN READ TAROT

While some tarot readers may be psychic on some level, psychic ability is not a prerequisite. With dedication and practice, anyone can learn to read cards. Tarot reading is a skill that can be developed, and intuitive abilities can be honed.

## MYTH - TAROT IS ASSOCIATED WITH EVIL/THE DEVIL

Tarot has a rich history rooted in esoteric spirituality, and as such has attracted the judgement of "evil" from those who seek to persecute spiritualities that differ from their own.

Tarot is literally an occult practice. Occult means "hidden" and for many, tarot is a hidden mystery. That said, unveiling these mysteries is not reserved for practitioners of esoteric religions. Tarot is a tool for self-discovery and personal growth, and can be used by people from any spiritual background. Whether a specific religion allows the use of the tarot is another matter entirely. That has nothing to do with tarot culture, but comes instead from the side of the opposing religious institution in question.

## MYTH - EACH CARD HAS A FIXED MEANING

Some believe that each tarot card has a rigid meaning. Yes, there are traditional meanings attached to each card, but these meanings are fluid and dynamic. Deck creators can and do create their own cards for the tarot and add entirely new elements to the tradition. Readers too can create their own meanings for any cards. Even when reading with traditional meanings, interpretations can vary based on context, surrounding cards, and the reader's perspectives on any given day. Like all languages, the language of tarot is a living, ever evolving thing.

## MYTH - TAROT READINGS SHOULD ALWAYS BE POSITIVE

Another misconception is that tarot readings should always be positive and uplifting. It would be nice if this was true, but like everything else in life, tarot has its shadow side.

Tarot reflects life in all of its complexities, light and dark, and readings can include both positive and challenging aspects. Any reader, however, can give a positive spin to even the darkest readings, for out of struggle comes growth. There's a Star after every Tower.

## MYTH - CARD MEANINGS ARE LITERAL

How many times have you seen a tarot reading in a movie where the Death card shows up and ominous music plays as the character is doomed? It's so common it's almost laughable.

The Death card is not a literal prediction of impending death. The King cards are not specifically referring to ruling men. The Sun does not refer to the actual sun. The Hierophant is not the Pope or a Bishop. The Hermit card is not specific instruction to run away and live in a cave (but you could if you wanted to!). No card needs to be interpreted literally and to do so denies the interpretive nuances that give tarot its power.

## MYTH - TAROT READINGS ARE QUICK FIXES

Some believe that tarot readings provide quick solutions to problems. They can, in theory, but most of the time, a tarot reading is a tool that prompts a long and potentially difficult process of reflection and insight. Even with quick spreads like single card draws, the interpretation and reflective process is intricate. Tarot offers hints and clues, not easy, one size fits all quick fixes.

## MYTH - TAROT CAN CONTROL OR MANIPULATE

Tarot is not a form of mind-control or manipulation. It is a reflective tool that offers insights into whatever situation you can think of. Decisions and actions based on those insights are entirely in the hands of the individual receiving the reading.

If a querent chooses to use the information in their reading to manipulate or control others, that has nothing to do with the cards. Similarly, if a reader chooses to manipulate the querent with their reading, that's a choice of the reader that was probably made before a card was even drawn. Tarot is not the manipulator, it's a neutral object.

## MYTH - YOU MUST FOLLOW A CERTAIN RELIGION OR SPIRITUAL TRADITION TO USE TAROT

Any person of any spiritual background can read tarot. It might not be allowed in certain religious doctrines, but in theory, any person can benefit from tarot's insight if they so choose.

You don't need any special training or initiation to be a tarot reader. There's no baptismal font or membership cards or secret passwords known only to the initiated few. All that's required is a deck and an open mind ready to look within.

## MYTH - TAROT HAS RULES

Tarot has been around for such a long time that it's easy to imagine that the practice comes with a set of rules and regulations governing its use.

There are traditions and guides and suggestions and what other tarot practitioners have done before you. But tarot has no rules.

Everything about tarot is completely up to you, the practitioner. The way you choose to interact with your cards today might not be the way you choose to interact with them tomorrow. You definitely do not need to read in any certain manner just because someone else does it that way.

You may choose everything from your deck to what the cards mean. Make up your own meanings, make up your own spreads. Many tarot practitioners even make up their own decks.

Everything is up to you. There is no right or wrong way to read tarot.

## MYTH - ORACLE AND TAROT DECKS ARE THE SAME THING

While both are used for cartomancy, tarot cards and Oracle cards are different. Oracle cards are similar in that they're beautiful cards with profound meaning and significance attached to the art, but Oracles don't have the traditional meanings or history that the tarot has. Oracles don't have a unified traditional symbolic system. There are no traditional numbers for an Oracle deck. Oracle cards are delightful and can provide profound insight, but they're not tarot.

The Lenormand is a similar tradition in that Lenormand decks are pictorial cards with meanings attached. They are used to prompt reflections and even predictions about everyday things, but again, it's a totally different tradition to the tarot.

~

# IS TAROT MAGICAL?

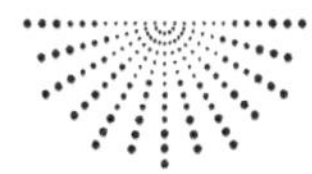

Is tarot actually magical?

Yes, some believe that tarot does indeed possess literal magical powers.

I believe tarot is what you make it. Tarot is what you want it to be. If you want it to be magical, it is. If you want it to be secular and neutral, then it is.

It's the meanings we ascribe to the cards, and how we use those meanings to prompt our thinking and explore our emotions, that gives tarot cards their power.

That said, I've had innumerable moments when I look at the cards I've drawn and marvel at how mystifyingly appropriate each card is in a spread. So often, I keep pulling the same cards, no matter how thoroughly I shuffled that deck. And that happens across different decks too, so it's not like a well-used deck might bring up the same cards thanks to some physical influence. There are some cards I rarely, if ever, draw.

Startling coincidences happen.

That's when the cards feel like magic.

As Albert Einstein said, "Coincidences are God's way of remaining anonymous." Maybe tarot is too.

# USING TAROT

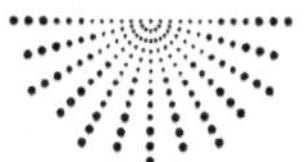

# CHOOSING A TAROT DECK

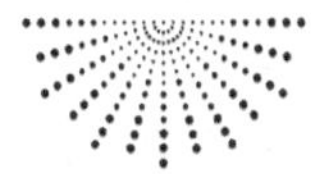

There are countless tarot decks to choose from.

Which one do you choose?

Where do you buy one?

Choosing your first deck is a bit like dating and falling in love. It's not a one size fits all approach. You keep an eye out for one you like the look of and ultimately choose the one you feel most connected to. It might be love at first sight, or there might be a getting to know you process. You might use a few decks before you find your perfect fit, and for some, there might be multiple true loves over time, and even multiple companions at the same time.

I own many decks. Some I use for reading, others I own because I like the images, others I own because they're traditionally significant decks and I don't feel a connection to the cards.

## THE RIDER-WAITE-SMITH DECK (RWS)

The Rider-Waite-Smith tarot is the classic deck, and the deck that most decks since the 1960s have been based on.

You might already be familiar with some of the imagery

from the RWS deck, as it's used all over pop culture, so it is a good starter option for many. I own the RWS deck simply to have it in my collection. I don't use it for readings, as I don't feel personally connected with the card imagery. That said, I do display a full wall sized artwork in my home of the complete RWS Major Arcana.

If you're serious about studying tarot traditions, familiarizing yourself with the RWS deck is recommended, but you don't have to use it for your readings.


## HOW TO CHOOSE A DECK

Don't overthink it. It's simple. Choose the deck that you like the look of. You don't have to wait for a bolt of lightning from the heavens to feel connected to a deck. Just pick the one that lights you up. There are so many decks in just about every theme imaginable. Magical and occult themes are prominent, for obvious reasons, and there are many spiritual decks around, like astrology decks, Zen decks, Qabala decks. You can even get Christian tarot cards–there's a Jesus deck or two, and plenty of angel themes.

There are dark decks with Gothic vibes, including vampires, Satanism, demonology, ghosts, and death, just to name a few. There are light decks. There are cat decks, cooking decks, knitting decks, sex decks, there's even a Gummy Bear deck. There are special interest decks like space and nature; decks from specific artists; native American arts; masculine and feminine decks; geographical decks, and alcohol themed decks. This list could go on and on and on. Whatever you're into, there will be a deck out there that feels like it was custom made just for you. I survey a selection of decks by theme on the Tarot Junction website and continue to add to this resource over time.

You can buy decks from a lot of different places. Bookstores often have them in the spirituality section, and you'll find them in new age and spiritual supplies stores.

You'll find the widest choices online. You'll find a great range of original and unique creations on Etsy. Many of these kinds of artisanal decks have a limited print run and sell out quickly. Kickstarter is another online source for new and exciting, limited edition decks. There are many mass produced decks available from all kinds of online stores, including Amazon.

In most stores, decks are sealed in plastic film. This makes it hard to get a feel for the cards and to see which imagery resonates. I've purchased a couple of decks I liked the look of from the samples on the box, only to get home to find the deck didn't excite me, and even disappointed me. I've also bought decks on a whim, liking the title cards on the box enough to pique my interest and got home to find I adore the entire deck more than I could ever imagine.

Because it can be tricky getting the vibe of a deck online and in some stores, I suggest checking out aecletctic.com, a website that reviews thousands of tarot decks and shows a lot of the images. You can also find deck walkthroughs on YouTube that show off the cards and whatever else comes in the deck pack.

Ultimately, you're never going to truly feel a deck until you have it in your hands, out of the box, so there might be a gamble in this initial introductory phase.


CARING FOR YOUR CARDS

Your tarot deck will not be just another one of your everyday possessions. It's not something to get shoved into a drawer, forgotten, and left to dust over. To get the most out of your practice, your tarot deck is a possession to be treasured and should be treated with a certain reverence.

Caring for your tarot deck is not just a matter of preserving the physical condition of the cards (though that's part of it). It's a ritual that fosters a connection between you and the tarot tradition. The more you feel a card deck means, the more it will mean, and taking care of your cards and handling them in a certain manner is a way to foster this bond.


**Handle Your Cards With Respect and Intention**

The energy exchange between you and your cards begins with touch. Handle them with care. The manner in which we physically connect with our cards can be an important part of the tarot ritual. Infuse your movements with intention. Each shuffle and draw is a conversation between you and the energies represented in the deck.


**Storing Your Deck**

Your tarot deck deserves a special place when not in use. Consider wrapping it in a special cloth or placing it in a dedicated box. Some practitioners even opt for wooden boxes or pouches adorned with crystals to enhance the deck's vibrational energy. Follow common sense practices, like keeping your cards away from direct sunlight and moisture.

I keep all of my decks arranged on a small table beside my desk. There are also a few Oracle decks, some affirmation cards, a small stereo, an aromatherapy diffuser, rune stones, a potted ivy, a lava lamp, and a picture of David Bowie as Jareth from *Labyrinth*. It's not any kind of altar, just a collection of things I like that add a certain vibe to my workspace, my special sanctuary in my home. I like to think my cards are happy there, and I certainly get a positive feeling when interact with the area.

**Cleansing and Clearing Energies**

Many believe that tarot cards absorb energy, both positive and negative, from their surroundings and their readings. As such, they cleanse their decks using methods like smoke bathing, placing the cards under moonlight, exposing them to sound energies, performing knocking rituals during shuffling, aligning them with specific crystals, saying spell incantations, affirmations, or meditating with the deck.

I don't perform any of these rituals myself, but feel the overall care and reverence I give my decks together with the intentional shuffling when I am starting a reading is enough to align the cards with my psyche.

**Addressing Wear and Tear**

Through regular use, any tarot deck will show signs of wear and tear. Embrace these signs as symbols of a well-loved tool rather than sad deterioration. If individual cards become damaged, they can be repaired. I recommend proper archival tools and materials, not just a strip of regular tape. Look into the kinds of tapes, glues and other materials used in libraries to repair books. Most high-quality decks will withstand years of regular use with little wear and tear. I've had some decks in use for multiple decades and they are still looking fine.

Many of these care practices might seem obvious, but it's important to remember that it's our intentions that imbue the cards with their power, and taking care of the cards and the way they're handled is a big part of that intention. The more you invest in the care of your tarot deck, the more it will give back during your readings.

## BONDING THROUGH REGULAR READINGS

Like any relationship, your connection with your tarot deck deepens with time and regular interaction. You might like to perform simple daily draws, even just one card. This practice also enhances your intuitive abilities and learning of the traditional meanings.

I often keep a card beside my bed. This could be from a single card draw, a particularly relevant card from a more complex draw, or a card that speaks to me in the moment. I also often accompany this card with an Oracle card from a complimenting deck.

For me, these cards are a reminder of an overarching theme or condition I'm trying to foster in life at the time, or perhaps also a reminder of what I need to do to look after myself, or address any specific problem.

## CREATING A TAROT READING SPACE

Reading tarot is not about the mere act of laying out cards and looking at pictures; it's an immersive experience that begins the moment you decide to engage with the deck.

Tarot reading is at its most powerful when performed with intention, and the space in which you perform your readings goes a long way to create that intention and foster a sense of ritual and significance within your practice.

Begin by selecting a space that resonates with you. It should be tranquil, inspiring, and protected from outside distractions. It could be a corner of a room, a special table, your bed, your garden, or any cozy nook somewhere in your home.

Infuse your space with personal elements that resonate

with your individuality. It could be symbols, artwork, crystals, or objects that hold personal significance. While these elements help to expand your personal energies, ensure the actual card reading space is free from clutter and distraction.

Many believe in the spiritual properties of crystals and or candles and incorporate these items into their tarot spaces to draw upon their power. You don't have to have a particular spiritual belief in crystals of candles to benefit from them, though. Their presence creates an aesthetic ambience, and that alone is enough to set your tarot mindset. Interacting with these objects too, such as lighting a candle or rubbing a crystal, can bring ritual to the tarot space, furthering your intentionality and deepening your connection with the cards.

Some practitioners prepare their space with special cleansing acts before they sit down to read. This is a lovely idea but is only necessary if you choose. I don't do anything so elaborate. I settled into my room, usually my bedroom or office, clear a space on my desk, bed, or the floor. A few centering breaths, and meditating on my situation as I shuffle the deck is enough to set me in the right physical and mental space.

You might like to perform your reading on a dedicated tarot cloth. This special cloth serves both practical and symbolic purposes. It provides a clean and uncluttered surface for your cards, and its material, color, or patterns can resonate with your personal energy or the themes of your readings. The act of spreading the cloth might become a ceremonial opening to your readings.

Some of the more elaborate deck packages come with cloths. Some decks come with thematically designed spread mats, depicting spaces for cards arranged in a particular spread such as The Celtic Cross.

In essence, your tarot space is the reflection of your intention, a sanctuary where you can slip away from the real world for a time and enter the energies of you and your life. It's entirely up to you how that works and what that looks like. All the above is a wonderful way to set the mood and your intention, but if you use tarot in some other way, that's perfectly fine too. Many a tarot reading has been done on the go, in a car, on a park bench, a coffee shop, and anywhere else you might imagine. The only wrong way to interact with tarot is in a way that doesn't feel good and right for you.

SHUFFLING

Some believe there are certain ways a tarot deck should be shuffled before the reading begins.

This is a matter of personal belief and preference.

Some shuffle in certain directions, split the deck in certain ways, or perform other symbolic practices such as kissing the cards or knocking on the pile. This is all fine and is a sweet way to infuse the practice with ritual and intention. Ultimately, however you choose to shuffle your cards is up to you. As always, there is no right or wrong way to do it.

I am a big fan of the all over the table or floor, messy mix form of shuffling a deck. I find it is a much more physical process rather than a normal hand shuffle, and as such, brings more of me into the session.

When reading for other people, you might like to involve them in the shuffle in various ways, such as getting them to start the shuffling, splitting the deck, or selecting a pile from a split deck to draw from.

# CONSULT THE BOOKS OR LEARN THE CARDS FROM MEMORY?

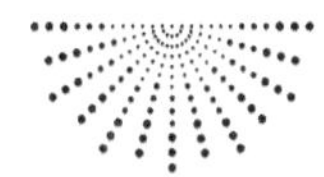

Do you need to memorize the traditional tarot meanings before you can start using the cards? Can you consult the books and other explanatory resources during a reading?

Even after decades of reading tarot, I still consult deck books and other printed resources at almost every read. I like to survey the cards first with my instinctive interpretations and then combine those with the traditional meanings of the cards.

There is absolutely nothing wrong with consulting the deck companion books, any other book, or a website as you're reading any spread.

While intuitive, off-the-cuff reading brings a beautiful personal meaning to a spread, using the traditional meanings and the interpretations of others grounds your experience in the ancient lore of tarot, layering on significances you might never have otherwise thought of on your own.

Plus, since many decks give new meanings to cards by working with all kinds of different visual symbolism, different decks will give differently nuanced readings. For example, a reading from the Thoth deck will take on an entirely different significance than a reading from a kitten deck, even if comparable cards are drawn. The deck's accompanying resources will guide you through these variations.

If you're just starting out with tarot, I recommend reading from your deck guidebook as well as looking up the classic RWS interpretations first. You might like to get started with my book, *Tarot Meanings: Traditional Tarot Meanings in Quick, Easy To Memorize Phrases.*

Many readers insist on memorizing every card's traditional meanings. You don't need to memorize anything, but if this is the way you want to read, then go for it. If you decide to learn the meanings off by heart, the manner in which you embark on that study is up to you. I know one reader who spent an entire week focusing on each card, and swears by her method. Others do a card a day. Some start with The Fool and move numerically through the deck, others go for the images they're drawn to first. If you're inclined to these kinds of methodical learning commitments, enjoy your journey. If you're not, just use the cards however you like and discern their meaning in the ways that work best for you.

# INTUITIVE READING

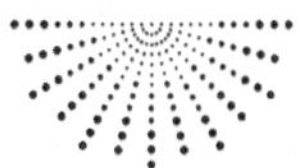

Intuitive reading is a conversation between the subconscious mind and the symbolic language of the cards. Intuitive tarot transcends structured meanings and invites readers to trust the guidance of their inner voices.

At its core, intuitive tarot involves tapping into one's innate instincts, emotions, and inner knowing. Rather than relying solely on predefined meanings and spreads, the reader allowing personal feelings and impressions to shape the reading.

## HOW TO DO AN INTUITIVE READING

Intuitive readings can be done in several ways.

You can use traditional spreads and infer intuitive readings from the cards. You could use intuitive spreads and rely on traditional meanings of the cards. You could use intuitive spreads and intuitive interpretations together, or, in the spirit of truly following your intuition, you could do whatever you feel like in the moment.

Lay out your cards in whatever spread pattern you choose.

When you reveal your cards, listen to and trust the subtle nudges, gut feelings, and immediate impressions that arise when a card is revealed.

Look at the title, the overall image, the details, the colors and other symbols, the numbers. How does it all make you feel? What does it make you think about? Do you like this card? Are you disappointed and were wishing for another card?

Just open yourself up to whatever is happening in your mind and body without judgement. It's okay to have a negative reaction. It's okay to have an ambivalent or completely blank reaction. It's all information.

In intuitive tarot reading, the visual elements of the cards are paramount. The imagery, symbolism, and emotional cues evoked by each card are the prompts a reader responds to in finding their answers. Our subconscious minds are primal and operate beyond language. Images are one such language that goes straight into this primal nature in a way that intellectual analysis alone cannot.

This act of surrendering to the flow of intuition fosters a unique and personal connection with the tarot, and allows it to probe the subconscious mind in a way that researching traditional meanings cannot. This invites a more organic and open-ended exploration of the matter you're reading for.


## MINDFULNESS AND INTUITIVE READING

Intuitive tarot reading thrives in the present moment. As such, intuitive tarot reading is a marvelous exercise in mindfulness. You're paying attention to what's happening in your mind and body as each card is revealed in the moment.

## COMBINING TRADITION AND INTUITION

While intuitive reading embraces the impulse of instinct, it doesn't negate the value of established tarot tradition. Often, readers who operate with this intuitive method are also using the traditional meanings of the cards (mostly derived from the RWS deck) they have committed to memory.

I do not believe it's even possible to get a truly independent response from a card if one knows even a little of its traditional meanings. Everything we see and do and learn is, after all, embedded in our spirits somewhere. So lean into that harmonious interplay of intuition and learned wisdom to create a truly unique reading.

## EMBRACING OTHER'S INTERPRETATIONS

While intuitive reading is profoundly personal, the practice brings limitless diversity to tarot. Two readers may draw the same card yet offer vastly different insights based on their intuitive connection. This acknowledgment of individual perspectives creates a rich array of meanings and fosters a diverse and endlessly fascinating tarot community.

## GETTING STARTED WITH INTUITIVE READING

Many new readers are intimidated by intuitive tarot reading. "What if I get it wrong?" is a common fear. Rest knowing that getting it wrong is actually impossible since there is no wrong way. Listen to your mind, your gut, your soul, the cards themselves, and you will instinctively know the right way to proceed.

# WHAT CAN TAROT BE USED FOR?

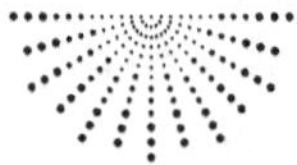

There is no limit to the things you can explore using tarot. The following section gives you some ideas on ways to use tarot in your life.

## SELF-REFLECTION

When you consult the cards using intentional questions and thoughtful interpretation, tarot offers you insights into your emotions, desires, and potentially hidden aspects of your psyche. This is an incredible way to get to know yourself, and I bet the cards will surprise you at every turn.

## ASKING QUESTIONS

Tarot is wonderful for answering both open-ended and concrete answer questions. Whether you're navigating challenges, seeking clarity on relationships, or exploring your life's purpose, practice asking questions of yourself in many different ways. Sometimes we can get fresh insights into the same problem by looking at it through the lens of a different question.

RECOGNIZING EMOTIONAL PATTERNS

As you practice with tarot, reflecting on what the cards tell you, you will probably recognize certain patterns arising, certain feelings that continue to occur. These emotional patterns are gold mines for internal introspection as the things that keep recurring are usually the major themes in our lives that need facing.

Once these emotional patterns are identified, we can address them, which means we can clear our blockages and uncover hidden strengths and potentials. This can be the case with both positive and negative emotions.

Allow the cards and your reactions to them to act as signposts, guiding you toward what you are actually feeling. How is that empowering or hindering you? Celebrate moments of triumph and joy, but also confront challenges and shadows with courage. Remember to treat your emotions and your emotional experiences with compassion and respect. Even the hard feelings are valuable.

TAROT JOURNALING

Journaling the outcomes of your readings is an excellent self-development practice. I have been journaling with tarot for decades and don't feel a reading is complete unless I have done a journaling session alongside it.

How I journal with tarot depends on how much time I have in any session, but it largely follows the same pattern. I start by a quick entry into my journal of what my intentions are with the coming read. As I shuffle the cards, I keep these intentions in mind.

I record the type of spread (three cards, Celtic Cross, etc), and then reveal the cards, noting in my journal what each card is and what the position of it represents. I then take time to freewrite on my intuitive reactions to the cards.

Following this, I write about what the card means from its traditional interpretations in the spread position and how that relates to my intuitive interpretations. I journal about each card individually as well as the overall spread arrangements. I then finish by writing a summary of what the spread has brought up, what it is taught me, and what I think it is asking of me.

I find this process solidifies my reading, clarifying my thinking and feeling more than reading with just the cards. Perhaps this is because I am a writer to my core and do my best thinking when putting words onto the page. Your experiences might be different.


## INTEGRATING TAROT INTO MEDITATION AND MINDFULNESS

Whether you're seeking clarity, peace, or a deeper connection with your intuition, the cards can be used as focal points, visualizations, or guides during your meditative or mindful moments.

Try focusing your thoughts in a meditation session on a particular card, or on the outcome of a spread. Alternatively, as you go about your day following a reading, try to remain mindful of how your actions and experiences are reflecting the messages from the cards.


## SETTING INTENTIONS WITH TAROT

Intentions shape our lives. Tarot can help set intentions in everything from the loftier experiences, right down to the day-to-day happenings.

What do you want to create in your life? Love? Money? Travel? Calm? Gratitude? Creativity? Whatever it is you intend, look for signs in your readings that offer advice on how to manifest these desires. Use the results of your reading to clarify your aspirations. If you have a positive emotional reaction to a reading, it's a good sign that you are on the right track and in alignment with your highest self. If you have a negative reaction to a reading, it can be a sign that you might not be entirely clear on your desires, or that the cards might be testing that clarity by suggesting the opposite.

Reading itself can be infused with intention. Be clear about what you are asking from the cards, and do it in a ritualistic manner. Your intention is to glean insight from the cards so make everything in your practice—the way you sit, the way you breathe, the way you hold the cards, the spread that you choose, and the way you think—intentionally reflect this intention.

# MAKING DECISIONS WITH TAROT

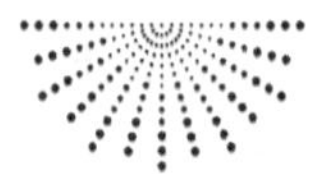

Whether you're grappling with major life choices or contemplating the next step on some small task, tarot can be your valuable companion and guide in the decision-making process.

A simple Yes No spread with a clear question is quite powerful. There is more on Yes No readings in the following section. Other times, we are looking for overview answers. In such cases, performing large and intricate spreads like The Celtic Cross with open-ended questions can also be used to guide decision-making.

There are many spreads specifically designed to make decisions and help you choose between different paths. You can consult one of the many tarot spread books, or do a quick google search for ideas. You might also like my book, ***Yes No Tarot: How To Make Decisions With Tarot.***

Your cards might point to specific outcomes of decisions chosen one way or the other (the spread will dictate this interpretation somewhat). They might also serve as warnings to heed if certain paths are followed in one direction over another. The cards might also show off alternatives, a kind of "Sliding Doors" effect, showing the outcomes of different paths taken, and let you make the choice depending on what feels like the best course of action. The cards might also show you important factors like when to act, which might be more important than the actual action taken. Often the cards can introduce other people into your decision-making, reminders of who your decision will affect outside of yourself, or where to seek support.

In all decision-making, whether or not we use tarot, the best decisions are made with a harmonious blend of logic and intuition. So don't forget to bring both into your reading, especially when deciding on life's big situations.


## YES NO ANSWERS

While some readers use tarot to explore multifaceted existential decisions, tarot is an excellent tool for basic binary Yes No answers. Sometimes we don't want or need a long and intricate analysis. Sometimes the power of tarot comes in the immediate revelation.

There are several ways to perform Yes No tarot readings. You can draw a single card and use reversals to show either yes or no. If the card is upright, the answer is a yes. If the card is reversed, the answer is a no.

Some readers use this technique in only looking at whether any card is upright or reversed regardless of what the card is. Some readers accept a yes or no answer from the card's direction and then use the meaning of the card to delve into the context of that yes or no answer.

Some yes or no tarot reading can go a little further with the reader drawing two cards, one for yes and one for no. The reader then analyzes the drawn cards as justifications for either a yes or a no sign, making their own choice somewhere in the middle of what the cards refer to.

# GOAL SETTING AND PLANNING WITH TAROT

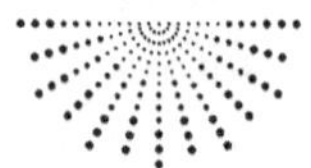

Whether your goals are for personal growth, career milestones, creative pursuits or anything else, tarot can help you align your aspirations with your intuition and your logic, infusing your plans with intention and clarity.

Goals shape our personal narratives, but they can be overwhelming and confusing. With the help of tarot, you can clarify what you're attempting to achieve, break down larger objectives into manageable steps, and take stock of your achievements along the way.

## CLARIFYING YOUR GOALS

Tarot can help you clarify your goals, providing insights into the challenges, opportunities, and potential outcomes tied to your desires.

If you're not sure of what your target is or might be, try these simple three card spreads to help to clarify your goals.

1. Where I have been.
2. Where I am.
3. Where I am going.

4. What I have.
5. What I want.
6. What I need.

Perhaps you are coming to your deck already with a goal in mind and are seeking help on how to further clarify things before you begin.

Try this three card spread.

1. Nature of previous goals that resulted in your present.
2. Nature of the goal in mind.
3. Prospects of the goal in mind.

More complex spreads can give more intricate readings.

With The Celtic Cross, for example, you can look to this new prospective goal within the context of your overall life. Or you can use it to focus on the goal itself in all of its many nuances, and how it will come to serve your life overall.

Try laying out cards in correspondence to other goal setting frameworks. For example, S.M.A.R.T goals are popular for some. It stands for Specific, Measurable, Achievable, Relevant, and Time Bound. The idea is that, to be worth your time and energy, your goals need to meet all the S.M.A.R.T criteria. Devise your own S.M.A.R.T spread where each card stands for each component of criteria.

## REFLECTING ON MOTIVATIONS

When we're thinking of new goals and we're feeling called to move in certain directions, it's sometimes easy to get caught up in the minutia of process and outcome and forget our Whys.

For goals to be successful, they all have to come with these motivational Whys, the reasons you're doing something.

Motivations fuel the pursuit of goals, and tarot can unveil the underlying driving forces and clarify your motivation.

Why do you truly want to pursue this goal?

The answer in your conscious mind might not be the same as the surprising revelation that your subconscious reveals in conversations with the cards.

Uncovering both conscious and subconscious motivations provides a holistic understanding of the forces at play in your actions and plans.

Try this three card Hidden Motivation spread:
1. What I am aiming for.
2. Why I think I want it?
3. Why I truly want it?

## IDENTIFYING STRENGTHS AND CHALLENGES

The pursuit of every goal is marked by strengths that propel us forward and challenges that test our resolve and threaten to derail us.

Tarot can identify both.

Try this simple spread
1. The nature of my goal.
2. My strengths that will help me get there.
3. What is holding me back?

## VISUALIZATION AND MANIFESTATION

Visualization is a potent ally in manifesting goals that can be enhanced by using tarot.

By creating visual representations of your goals through

the cards, you tap into the power of imagination and intention.

Draw cards intentionally to represent your goals. Or leave it up to your deck to decide how your goals are best represented.

Use these cards as mediation guides, visualizing your goal becoming reality. Then use these visions to direct your manifestation practices.

Remember, manifestation, visualization, and intention setting only work when combined with inspired action. You have to actually *DO* something to reach your goals, not just sit back and wait for the universe to deliver the results. Which is where inspired planning can come into play.

## CREATING INSPIRED ACTION PLANS

Goals are one thing, but goals only come to fruition through actionable steps. After all, the only difference between a dream and a goal is an action plan to get there. Tarot can help create practical action plans that align with your most fundamental needs as well as your most lofty desires.

Try this intuitive spread. With a goal already in mind, draw cards to illuminate your path of next right steps. Draw as many cards as you need until it feels right and you feel an innate knowing that it's time to begin with that first step, trusting you're heading in the right direction.

## ADAPTING TO CHANGE AND FLEXIBILITY

The journey towards any goal is dynamic, marked by twists and turns. This holds many people back, as there is a widespread belief that once you have a plan, it's set in stone. Not allowing for flexibility within that plan is the cause of many a goal's failure.

Tarot, with its fluid nature, excels in navigating this variability and helps us adapt to change.

When a shift occurs in pursuit of your goal, use tarot to explore the nature of that shift. Why is it happening (if there is a why at all)? Is it possible to bring things back on track? What's the new next right step to take in this new situation?

Try this simple, four card spread, laying the cards in whatever order feels right.

1. Previous path
2. Turning point
3. Reason for the shift
4. New path

## RECOGNIZING ACHIEVEMENTS

For some of us, when we're on the path towards goals and desires, it's easy to forget to reflect on and celebrate how far we've come. You might like to use tarot to help you truly see your milestones and achievements. This also helps cultivate a sense of gratitude for all that has brought you to this point.

# TAROT FOR CREATIVE INSPIRATION

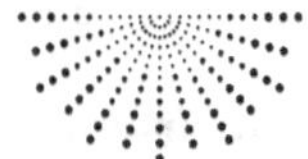

The bottomless inspirational energy of tarot goes hand in hand with the creative energy that dwells in each of us.

Whether you're a formal creative person like an artist, a writer, or a musician, or you're simply exploring what creative sparks might be smoldering in your depths, tarot is the perfect tool to help set those sparks into a blaze.

## UNCOVERING YOUR CREATIVITY

If you're feeling the need to explore your creativity and are not sure where to start, consult your cards.

Use a deck with art that particularly appeals to you. Don't overthink it. If you're not sure why you're drawn to the Thoth deck, for example, then just let yourself be drawn to it. If you find a surprising connection to the particular art in a deck about tea, then let that happen too, and embrace it. The art is already trying to tell you something.

More intuitive layouts can be helpful in delving into your creative urges, especially if you haven't explored yourself in this way before.

Start with one card. What does it make you feel and think? How is your curiosity sparked? Curiosity is a key to creative exploration, so listen to where it is leading you.

Keep on pulling cards until it feels right.

Journaling is helpful in this process, especially if your creative sparks drift toward the literary realms.


## EXPLORING YOUR CREATIVITY

You might already be familiar with your creative spirit and want to use tarot to find new ways to push yourself into new curiosities and potentials.

Do you have a new art project in mind? Perform a reading for that specifically.

If you've got the urge to create something but you're not sure how that will turn out, or what it will even be (a song, a painting, a story, etc.) then draw a card intuitively. Keep drawing cards until you feel the full shape of something form in your mind.


## WORKING WITH EXISTING CREATIVE PROJECTS

Tarot can be used in the actual creative process in many ways.

Perhaps it's you, the artist and Creatrix, who needs the clarifying insight. Perhaps it's the project yourself.

You might be blocked on a project, or perhaps just unsure where you're heading with it. Ask the cards.

You might question your motivations on the project, which is stalling your progress. Or perhaps you're unsure of the relevancy of this project in your overall life. Ask the cards.

You can also ask the cards to help you with the creation of your work, rather than its role in your life.

Tarot cards make excellent writing prompts. Or perhaps

an image strikes you in a way that you see a new style to bring into your own visual art. Try drawing a single card and looking at the art itself for your burst of inspiration, not so much the traditional meanings ascribed to that card.

Many writers read tarot for characters in their stories, using the cards as a writing companion to fuel their inspiration.

The possibilities here are endless and endlessly exciting.

## CREATING CREATIVE RITUALS

Creative rituals infuse intention into creative practices, and go a long way in solidifying creative habits and mindsets. We're not here specifically referring to a spiritual or religious ritual such as a prayer or an incantation. Rather, the word ritual is used here to refer to any intentional process we undertake as part of our creative practice that is not actually a part of the creation itself.

The writer who brews a cup of coffee before a writing session is engaging in a ritual. The musician who polishes their guitar before every session is engaging in a ritual. The artist who takes three deep breaths before they start painting is performing in a ritual. The power of a creative ritual is that the actions help to signal to the brain that the creator is about to enter creative flow, a different mode of thinking, feeling, and existing.

The possibilities for creative rituals are endless, and tarot can be a beautiful part of any artist's creative ritual. Perhaps you will pre-start your creative sessions by shuffling your deck and drawing a card. This card might set you tone for the session or advise on what you might be on the lookout for today, either in your work or yourself. You might have a specific question to ask the cards about the work you are facing in your session. Or you might simply draw a card and let the relevance of that card evolve as you move through the creative flow.

Tarot is born in creativity. The cards themselves are products of a creative spirit. The stories within the cards are the stories in each of us, and they all tell of birth and regeneration, and that is the truest story of all creation.

# WORKING WITH TRADITIONAL SPREADS

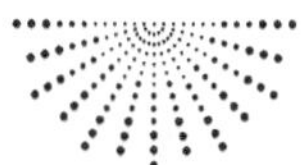

There are a number of classic spreads that tarot practitioners have been returning to for generations.

These traditions are a wonderful way to start a tarot practice, and keep on using as your relationship with the cards develops.

But, you might wonder, if the tarot is so personal, why would you use traditional spreads and not lay the cards out in your own ways?

As with everything in tarot, it's all up to you. Many readers use only traditional spreads, many use only their own spreads, many use a combination of both. This is how I work.

Traditional tarot spreads serve as a connection to the generations of tarot traditions that each of us builds upon. They are experienced guides that have endured the test of time. For me, working with the foundations of tradition, even if I'm making up something totally new and modern, adds further layers of significance and meanings to my practice and the insights I gain from each draw.

There's nothing stopping you from adding your own spin on the traditions of established spreads. You might add or subtract your own card positions or change the meanings of what a position signifies.

Embracing the structure of the traditional spreads, while simultaneously allowing room for intuition and spur-of-the-moment ideas, is one of the most potent ways to become a skilled tarot reader. Your personal spin on established customs adds another layer to that tradition. Just by picking up a deck of cards, each of us contributes to the living and ever evolving traditions of tarot.

The following sections explain a selection of the most common traditional tarot spreads.


## THE CELTIC CROSS

The Celtic Cross is a hallmark tarot spread. It comprises two sections: the cross itself, also called the circle, and the staff, also called the ladder.

The cross section (the first six cards) represents the nature of a problem, and the querent's life in general. In the center of the circle are two overlapping cards, the core cross. These represent the root nature of the problem, the essence of the question the querent brings to the table. The four cards of the ladder represent the nature of the solution, and a sign of what might happen if the querent continues on their current path.

The Celtic Cross is vast. This spread can apply to a deeply nuanced read of one situation, or it can be used as an analytical overview of life.

One of my favorite personal tarot traditions is performing a Celtic Cross spread every New Year's Day, asking the cards what I can look forward to in the coming year. I also like to do the same on my birthday. Given my birthday is almost exactly in the middle of the year, it's a nice even framing.

# CELTIC CROSS
## Traditional Spread

**The Celtic Cross Spread Labels**

There's a general established tradition of what each card represents in a Celtic Cross, but you will find many books and guides alter these position labels slightly.

I use the following position labels from Anna Marie Ferguson. It was her *Legend* deck I truly began my lifelong practice with.

Significator - a card specifically chosen to represent the querent. An optional card.

1. The querent in relationship to the present situation.
2. Positive forces in their favor (or a negative obstacle in the way).
3. Potential and aspirations. Also, a message from the "higher self".
4. Preoccupation of the subconscious.
5. Past events and influences.
6. Relationships with others.
7. Psychological state and attitudes.

8. Environment and unseen forces.
9. Hope and fears.
10. The Outcome.

Brigit Esselmont of Biddy Tarot uses the following Celtic Cross positions:

1. The Present.
2. The Challenge.
3. The Past.
4. The Future.
5. Above.
6. Below.
7. Advice.
8. External Influences.
9. Hopes and Fears.
10. Outcome.

Theresa Reed, The Tarot Lady, uses the following Celtic Cross positions.

1. The present moment.
2. What crosses you, for good or ill, an obstacle or support.
3. Foundations of the problem, the past.
4. Recent events, lingering effect.
5. On the horizon.
6. The near future.
7. Querent at the present moment.
8. Environment and surrounding influences.
9. Hopes and fears.
10. Outcome.

You might like to devise a personal custom Celtic Cross.

Reading the Celtic Cross can be as complicated or as simple as you like. You can read each position as separate, or you can look at how other cards might land to alter the meaning of the surrounding cards, interpreting the cross as a whole tapestry of meaning.

THREE CARD SPREADS

The three card spread is exactly what is sounds like, three cards. Don't let the simplicity fool you though. There is so much insight to be gained in the arrangements of three cards.

Different practitioners give different labels to a three card spread. Past, present, and future is one of the most common. You can apply this to your question, or to yourself. I also like problem, action, outcome applied to specific situations.

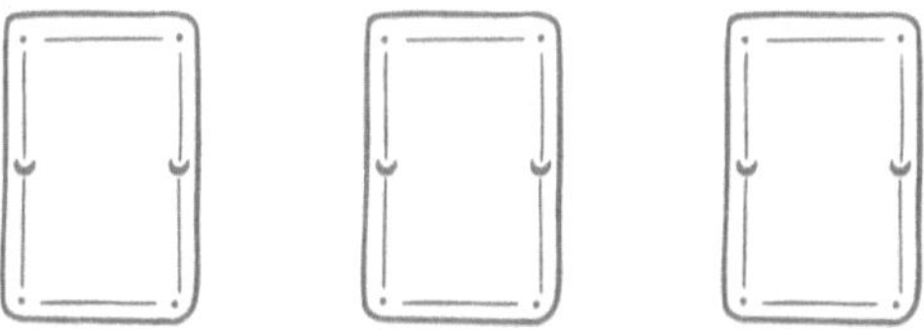

# THREE CARD SPREADS

1. Past.
2. Present.
3. Future.

1. Problem.
2. Action.
3. Outcome.


1. Origin of the problem.
2. Present effect of the problem.
3. Solution to the problem.


1. Past me.
2. Present me.
3. Future me.

The options of three card spread positioning are enormous. Have fun with it and play around with devising your own position labels.


## THE HORSESHOE SPREAD

The Horseshoe Spread is as a simplified iteration of the ideas explored in the Celtic Cross Spread, making it a favored choice for both those who are new to tarot readings, and well-practiced readers alike.

Here are the most common position labels of the Horseshoe spread:

1. Past.
2. Present.
3. Future.
4. Attitude toward the situation.
5. Other influences.
6. Obstacles.
7. Outcome.

# HORSESHOE
Traditional Spread

# CREATING YOUR OWN TAROT SPREADS

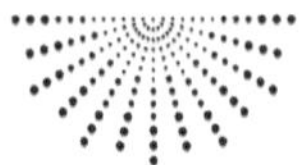

As you dig deeper into the world of tarot and refine your skills, you may find it worthwhile to create personalized spreads tailored to your specific needs. Like all tarot practices, this process relies on your intuition and what resonates with you at any given moment.

Set aside a peaceful moment for yourself, free from distractions. While shuffling your deck, contemplate the particular aspect of your life you wish to explore. Consider the key elements of the situation and the fundamental questions that arise within you.

Are you seeking definitive answers, or simply seeking flashes of insight to ignite your inspiration?

Before commencing the spread, you can determine the number of cards you wish to draw, perhaps even jotting them down in your tarot journal. Alternatively, you may choose to lay the cards intuitively as you go along, relying on what feels right.

Your arrangement of cards can hold symbolic significance. For instance, cards representing the future may be placed on the right side (as we read from left to right in English). Alternatively, a central concern could be positioned at the top or in the middle of the spread. Consider the ladder portion of the traditional Celtic Cross spread, where the final four cards are read upward towards the outcome card, resembling a journey of ascension through the reading. Allow yourself to have fun and embrace creativity when arranging your cards.

It's advisable to document the meanings of each card position in your custom spreads, ensuring you have a reference for future use.

In all spreads, the specific placement of the cards holds secondary importance. Yes, it serves as an additional layer of symbolism that can enhance your tarot reading experience, but ultimately, the choice of how and why you arrange the cards is entirely yours, and these preferences can always change. Trust in yourself, trust in the cards.

# WHAT TO DO WHEN A TAROT READING DOESN'T FEEL RIGHT

There come times where traditional and even intuitive card meanings just don't fit. They don't feel right, or we can't see how it all fits together.

What happens if you just can't draw a connection to the meaning, or if what the card is downright wrong for you and your question?

Here's an example situation:

Say you're worried about finances. You've got a cash flow problem and can't figure out any way to cut any more from your spending, and can't figure out a way to bring in any extra income.

You ask the cards for guidance.

You might expect to see a lot of Pentacles cards, the suit associated with money and other traditionally materialistic worldly manners. Perhaps you want to see cards that speak to abundance like the Empress or something like the Nine of Cups, (also known as The Wish Card), that speaks to receiving all kinds of blessings.

These types of cards would make perfect sense in a reading about money. Even negative cards like The Tower could apply with the right framing.

Instead, you draw the Ace of Cups, a card that is the essence of emotion, and the Four of Wands that's all about celebration, and The Devil. How on earth do these cards apply to your financial situation?

You consider the Devil. Maybe you're trapped by materialism and excess and it's a sign to give something up? But what if that's just not you? What if you're frugal and already restrict indulgences?

The guidance from the cards might come from your negative reaction to them, not the cards themselves. That Devil card, your conflicting reaction to it, along with its fellow cards might say: "it's not you that's the problem here, it's the economy, so lighten up on yourself, shake off this lack mindset, and look to how you feel and what there is to celebrate in life."

If you intuitively react negatively to a card and can't see how it applies, consider the reasons it doesn't fit. Find your answers in the opposite of what the card is suggesting. Tarot is always a prompt and sometimes those inspired ideas and answers can come through a process of lateral thinking.

# TAROT READER'S BLOCK

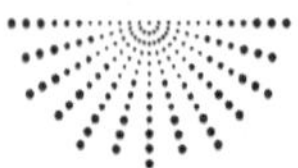

Tarot reader's block is the feeling when you can't connect to your cards. It might start out with you just feeling like the cards don't apply. You do the mindset shifts mentioned in the previous section, even so, you fail to draw meaning out of your cards, and you're just not feeling it.

There are many reasons for reader's block. Perhaps you're tired. Perhaps you're hungry. Perhaps there is something else going on in your life that is disrupting you and you can't find a place of rested mindfulness in which to connect with the cards and your inner wisdom. Perhaps there's something in your environment that is distracting you. Whatever is at the heart of the block, the solutions are generally similar.

Take a break. Get something to eat. Make sure that you're hydrated. Perhaps come back tomorrow after you've slept and are feeling more rested. Try cleansing yourself, physically or spiritually, for the session. You might also like to consider grounding activities such as meditation candle rituals, or simply getting outside for a walk. You might like to take your cards out into the garden, or go into your bedroom and close the door, or some other way to change up your reading environment. You might even like to try a different deck.

It might be the case where we must accept that there is a significant psychic distraction going on in life and sit with that. Accept that it is interrupting your reading. Don't stress about it. Just come back to the cards when you're feeling more centered.

Tarot reader's block might also be a sign that you are not trusting yourself, at least not at this moment. If you look within and find that you do want to read, that you do trust yourself, then it might be a simple case of waiting. Perhaps a few hours, perhaps the next day, your situation may feel differently.

Ultimately, there will not be one fix that will suddenly clear your reader's block. Like any other form of creative block, it usually stems from a place of depletion. So do what you need to do to replenish, whether that's sleep, food, exercise, or going away to do something completely different for a while, and coming back to try again later.

The important thing to remember is not to despair. Reader's block is not permanent, it's rarely even long-lasting. Since there's usually some form of stress involved (physical, emotional, environmental), getting worked up about being blocked is only going to make your stress worse. So relax, rest and come back to your cards again tomorrow. They will wait for you.

# CONTINUING YOUR TAROT JOURNEY

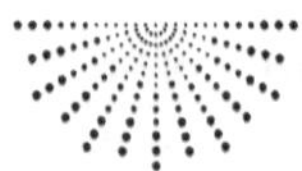

Tarot is a perpetually unfolding journey. There is no ultimate moment where you grasp every nuance and have finally, once and for all, learned to read tarot. Meanings continuously emerge. Your intuition, woven with the fabric of your experiences, is always changing, and there are always more decks to guide you through your development. It's no wonder why countless practitioners, myself included, collect numerous decks along our way.

Tarot changes. A spread cast on one day may unveil entirely different insights on another, even with the exact same cards in hand.

Tarot also stays the same. As you delve into readings, take note of recurring cards. I, and so many others, see identical cards surface across various readings, spanning diverse decks. It might be coincidence. It feels like magic. How might these recurrences change with you over time?

Whether you read tarot casually or immerse yourself entirely in the tarot world, whether you go fully intuitive, or rely solely on the traditional ways, whether you learn the cards by rote or only rely solely on guidebooks, you are still a tarot practitioner. Your journey is the right journey.

Embrace yourself.

# ABOUT THE AUTHOR

Kat Elmwood (she/her) is a lifelong tarot devotee.

Kat has practiced tarot for over thirty years and has had a deck on hand for every life stage.

She is an author in multiple genres (fiction and nonfiction) under multiple pennames, an artist, a mother, and many other titles.

Kat's current favorite tarot deck is *The Wandering Star Tarot* by Cat Pierce.